**IREDELL COUNTY PUBLIC LIBRARY**
www.iredell.lib.nc.us

# A Guide to AMERICAN STATES

# Arkansas

## THE NATURAL STATE

MEDIA ENHANCED BOOKS
AV²
BY WEIGL
ADDED VALUE · AUDIO VISUAL

www.av2books.com

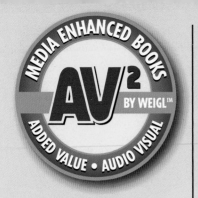

AV² provides enriched content that supplements and complements this book. Weigl's AV² books strive to create inspired learning and engage young minds in a total learning experience.

## Your AV² Media Enhanced books come alive with...

**Audio**
Listen to sections of the book read aloud.

**Key Words**
Study vocabulary, and complete a matching word activity.

Go to **www.av2books.com**, and enter this book's unique code.

**Video**
Watch informative video clips.

**Quizzes**
Test your knowledge.

## BOOK CODE

**W 1 7 1 7 4 2**

**Embedded Weblinks**
Gain additional information for research.

**Slide Show**
View images and captions, and prepare a presentation.

**AV² by Weigl** brings you media enhanced books that support active learning.

**Try This!**
Complete activities and hands-on experiments.

**... and much, much more!**

Published by AV² by Weigl
350 5th Avenue, 59th Floor
New York, NY 10118
Website: www.av2books.com    www.weigl.com

Copyright 2012 AV² by Weigl
All rights reserved. No part of this publication may be reproduced, stored in a retrieval system, or transmitted in any form or by any means, electronic, mechanical, photocopying, recording, or otherwise, without the prior written permission of the publisher.

Library of Congress Cataloging-in-Publication Data

Pezzi, Bryan.
 Arkansas / Bryan Pezzi.
    p. cm. -- (A guide to American states)
 Includes index.
 ISBN 978-1-61690-776-1 (hardcover : alk. paper) -- ISBN 978-1-61690-451-7 (online)
 1. Arkansas--Juvenile literature. I. Title.
 F411.3.P495 2011
 976.7--dc22
                          2011018315

Printed in the United States of America in North Mankato, Minnesota

052011
WEP180511

Project Coordinator  Jordan McGill
Art Director  Terry Paulhus

Photo Credits
Every reasonable effort has been made to trace ownership and to obtain permission to reprint copyright material. The publishers would be pleased to have any errors or omissions brought to their attention so that they may be corrected in subsequent printings.

Weigl acknowledges Getty Images as its primary image supplier for this title.

# Contents

Blanchard Springs Cavern is a popular tourist attraction. The entrance to the cave is almost 200 feet underground. Visitors are able to see a 70-foot column and walk across a natural bridge.

# Introduction

A rkansas is known for its Southern charm and natural wonders. In fact, its nickname is "the Natural State." Arkansas has rugged mountains, clear lakes and streams, and an abundance of wildlife. The southwest is known for its oil fields and grazing cattle, and the northwest is characterized by dairy farms and orchards. In the east, near the Mississippi River, are cotton **plantations** like those of other states of the Deep South. Over the past 500 years Arkansas has developed from a vast wilderness to a modern, progressive state. Its economy includes agriculture, technology, and commerce. Arkansas has a wealth of natural resources, but its friendly people are its greatest asset.

Arkansas is one of the largest producers of cotton in the United States.

Arkansas has the only diamond mine still active in the United States.

The name Arkansas reflects the early influence of American Indian and French cultures in the area. French explorers discovered a group of American Indians of the Quapaw tribe that they called the Arkansea, a name other local Indians used for the Quapaws that means "People of the South Wind." "Arkansea" eventually was modified slightly to "Arkansas." For many years residents disagreed about how the word should be pronounced. Some people said AR-kan-SAW, while others insisted it was Ar-KANSAS. In 1881 the state's General Assembly decided that the name would be spelled "Arkansas" but pronounced "Arkansaw." Throughout its history, Arkansas has gained many nicknames in addition to the Natural State. As early as 1875 the state was billed as the Land of Opportunity in an effort to attract new residents. Some people call Arkansas the Hot Water State for its many hot springs.

# Where Is Arkansas?

**A**rkansas is located in the western portion of the south-central part of the United States, just west of the Mississippi River. Visitors can travel to Arkansas by car, bus, plane, or train. Major transportation routes pass through Little Rock, the state's capital and largest city. Interstates 40 and 30 lead to Little Rock, as do U.S. Highways 65 and 67. Most major domestic airlines touch down and take off at Little Rock National Airport, which serves almost 3 million travelers each year.

The skyline of Little Rock features several of the tallest buildings in the state.

Arkansas has some other big cities spread around the state. Fort Smith, Arkansas's second-largest city, is located about 160 miles west of Little Rock, near the Oklahoma border. Almost 60 miles to the north of Fort Smith is Fayetteville, home of the University of Arkansas. Less than 10 miles north of Fayetteville is Springdale, a center for meat processing. In the northeast is Jonesboro, where Arkansas State University is located. Texarkana is in the far southwest, right on the Texas border. Pine Bluff is an agricultural center about 45 miles southeast of Little Rock.

# I DIDN'T KNOW THAT!

**With a total area** of 53,179 square miles, Arkansas is the 29th largest state.

**Arkansas has a pledge** to the state flag: "I Salute the Arkansas Flag with Its Diamond and Stars. We Pledge Our Loyalty to Thee."

**Lake Ouachita** is the largest lake in Arkansas. It is a human-made reservoir created by the damming of the Ouachita River.

*Fayetteville is located in northwestern Arkansas. Thousands of people flock to the city to watch the University of Arkansas Razorbacks football team play at Donald W. Reynolds Razorback Stadium.*

# Mapping Arkansas

**A**rkansas is bordered by six other states. In the east the Mississippi River separates Arkansas from both Tennessee and Mississippi. Missouri lies to the north of Arkansas, and Louisiana lies to the south. Oklahoma and Texas border Arkansas to the west.

## Sites and Symbols

**STATE SEAL**
Arkansas

**STATE BIRD**
Mockingbird

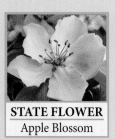

**STATE FLOWER**
Apple Blossom

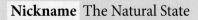

**STATE FLAG**
Arkansas

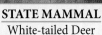

**STATE MAMMAL**
White-tailed Deer

**STATE TREE**
Pine

**Nickname** The Natural State

**Motto** *Regnat Populus* (The People Rule)

**Song** "Arkansas," by Eva Ware Barnett; "Arkansas (You Run Deep in Me)," by Wayland Holyfield; "Oh, Arkansas," by Terry Rose and Gary Klaff; "The Arkansas Traveler," words by the Arkansas State Song Selection Committee, music by Colonel Sanford Faulkner

**Entered the Union** June 15, 1836, as the 25th state

**Capital** Little Rock

**Population** (2010 Census) 2,915,918 Ranked 32nd state

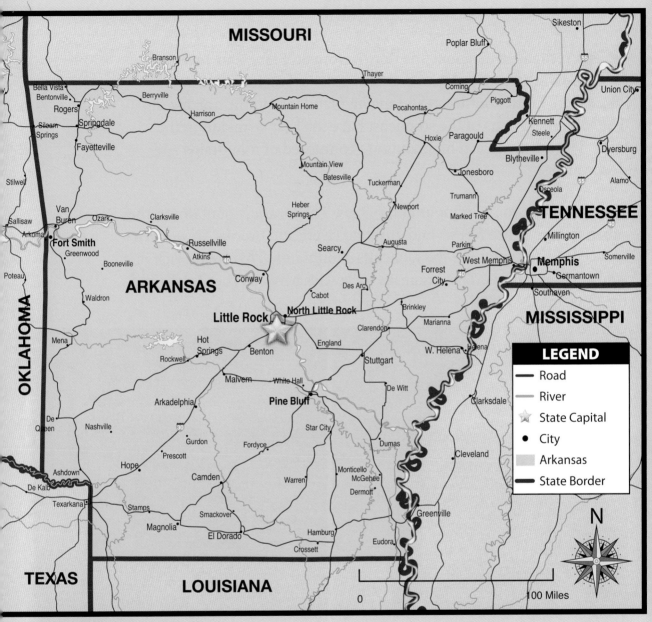

MISSOURI

Sikeston
Poplar Bluff
Branson
Thayer
Bella Vista
Bentonville
Rogers
Berryville
Corning
Piggott
Union City
Siloam
Springs
Springdale
Harrison
Pocahontas
Kennett
Steele
Fayetteville
Mountain Home
Hoxie
Paragould
Dyersburg
Mountain View
Jonesboro
Blytheville
Osceola
Alamo
Stilwell
Batesville
Tuckerman
Trumann
Van
Buren
Ozark
Clarksville
Heber
Springs
Newport
Marked Tree
TENNESSEE
Sallisaw
Arkoma
Fort Smith
Greenwood
Russellville
Atkins
Searcy
Augusta
Parkin
Millington
Somerville
Poteau
Booneville
Conway
Des Arc
West Memphis
Memphis
Germantown
ARKANSAS
Waldron
Cabot
Forrest
City
North Little Rock
Little Rock
Brinkley
Southaven
Mena
Clarendon
Marianna
MISSISSIPPI
Hot
Springs
Benton
England
W. Helena Helena
Rockwell
Stuttgart
Malvern
White Hall
De Witt
Clarksdale
Arkadelphia
Pine Bluff
De
Queen
Nashville
Star City
Cleveland
Gurdon
Fordyce
Dumas
Prescott
Ashdown
Hope
Camden
Warren
Monticello
McGehee
De Kalb
Dermott
Texarkana
Stamps
Smackover
Greenville
Magnolia
El Dorado
Hamburg
Eudora
Crossett
TEXAS
LOUISIANA

OKLAHOMA

LEGEND
— Road
— River
⭐ State Capital
• City
  Arkansas
— State Border

N

0          100 Miles

# STATE CAPITAL

The capital of Arkansas is Little Rock. It is located in Pulaski County on the south bank of the Arkansas River, near the geographical center of the state. The western part of Little Rock lies in the foothills of the Ouachita Mountains. Founded in 1821, the city now offers a mix of old and new architecture that includes ornate 19th-century buildings and modern glass-faced skyscrapers.

## United States

Hawai'i  Alaska

Arkansas

# The Land

On a map, a diagonal line drawn from St. Francis to Texarkana divides Arkansas into two triangular segments. The lowlands are in the southeast, and the highlands are in the northwest. The low, level plains of the southeast have the best farmland in the state. The northwestern highlands are composed of mountains and deep valleys.

Arkansas has two main mountain ranges. The Ozark Mountains in the north feature dense forests and gurgling rivers and brooks. In western and central Arkansas are the Ouachita Mountains. This area is rich in coal and natural gas. The Arkansas Valley lies between the Ozarks and the Ouachita Mountains.

## OZARK MOUNTAINS

The Ozark Mountain region is filled with scenic peaks, as well as lush forests, clear-running streams and a variety of caves and underground caverns.

## LAKE CHICOT

Lake Chicot is the state's largest natural lake. Its name, which means "stumpy" in French, describes the many cypress tree stumps that line the lake's banks.

## OUACHITA MOUNTAINS

The Ouachita Mountains in western Arkansas are one of two mountain ranges in the country that run east to west, rather than north to south. Visitors to the area can enjoy rugged trails, scenic vistas, and clear lakes.

## MAGAZINE MOUNTAIN

Magazine Mountain is the state's highest point at 2,753 feet above sea level. The peak is located in western Arkansas between the Ouachita Mountains and the Ozark Plateau.

**The Mississippi River** forms Arkansas's border with its eastern neighbors, Tennessee and Mississippi. The state's other major rivers include the Arkansas, the Ouachita, the Red, the White, and the St. Francis.

**Mammoth Spring** in northeastern Arkansas is the largest spring in the state. Nine million gallons of water pour out of the spring each hour, forming a 10-acre lake that then flows south as the Spring River.

*Tornadoes occur an average of 26 times each year in Arkansas, although in 1999 a record 107 of the destructive windstorms touched down in the state.*

# Climate

A rkansas's climate is warm and wet. Summers are long and hot, with temperatures occasionally rising above 100° Fahrenheit. Typically, July temperatures soar to about 80° F. Winters are short and mild. January temperatures average about 42° F. Annually, Arkansas averages 50 inches of rainfall and 6 inches of snowfall.

With mountains in the northwest and low-lying plains in the southeast, the state's varied landscape can sometimes produce weather extremes that are most common in the spring and fall. In addition, Arkansas's geographic location makes it prone to tornadoes.

## Average Annual Temperatures Across Arkansas

The average annual temperatures in Fayetteville, Jonesboro, Little Rock, and Texarkana all fall between about 58° F and 65° F. Why do you think temperatures do not vary too much around the state?

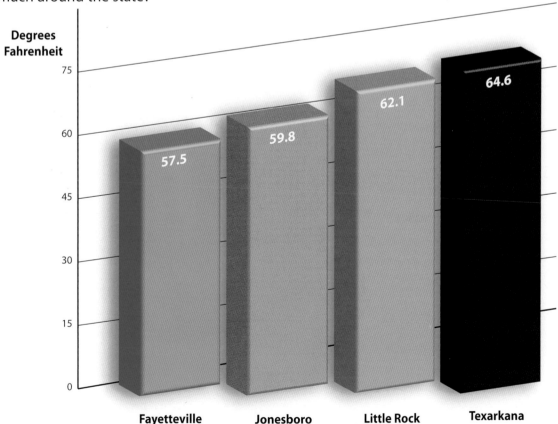

# Natural Resources

Nature has blessed Arkansas with many resources. Arkansas was the first state to mine diamonds. Diamond mining began in 1906, when John Huddleston spotted two of the glittering stones in the dirt on his farm in southwestern Arkansas. His land became the only diamond mine in the country at the time. Today visitors can search for diamonds at Crater of Diamonds State Park in Murfreesboro. They can even keep any diamonds they find while digging! More than 75,000 diamonds have been found in Crater of Diamonds State Park.

Quartz crystal is another important mineral found in Arkansas. These crystals are sometimes called "Arkansas diamonds," but they are not true diamonds. Quartz crystals are mined in the Ouachita Mountains and are used in computer components. This stone became Arkansas's state mineral in 1967.

The 40-carat "Uncle Sam" diamond is the largest diamond ever found in the United States. It was unearthed in 1924 near Murfreesboro.

Oil and natural gas are both important resources in the state. The production of natural gas has undergone a large increase during recent years. Petroleum production has decreased but remains significant.

## I DIDN'T KNOW THAT!

**Arkansas is the top** bromine producer in the United States. This element is used in dyes and medicines.

**Saline County** is home to the largest bauxite deposits in the United States. Bauxite is used to make aluminum.

**The state leads** the United States in the production of silica stone, which is used as an abrasive.

**Crater of Diamonds State Park** in Murfreesboro is the only active diamond mine in the United States. Visitors can search for diamonds at the site. An average of two of the precious gems are found at the park each day.

*Petroleum is among the top minerals produced in Arkansas. All of the state's oil production occurs in Arkansas's southern region.*

# Plants

The Natural State lives up to its nickname. Approximately half of Arkansas is wooded. Forests and natural areas provide habitats for many plant species.

There are many forested areas in Arkansas's mountains. Hardwood forests of oak, hickory, maple, and beech stretch across the Ozarks. In the Ouachita Mountains shortleaf pine forests thrive. Pine forests are also common in southern Arkansas.

Arkansas's eastern border is part of the Mississippi Delta region. Swamps and **bayous** support cypress trees and water tupelos.

Many varieties of brightly colored and sweet-smelling flowers bloom in most parts of the state. Passionflowers, water lilies, and orchids grow in Arkansas. There are many different kinds of wildflowers found in the forested areas, including American bellflowers, asters, verbenas, phlox, and wild hydrangeas.

**PINE TREES**

The pine is the state tree. Two varieties, loblolly and shortleaf, are found in the state. Both can grow to be 100 feet tall.

**APPLE BLOSSOMS**

The apple blossom is Arkansas's state flower. It has pink and white petals. At one time Arkansas was a major apple-producing state.

## INDIAN PAINTBRUSHES

Indian paintbrush is a wildflower that frequently is found in rocky areas of the Ozark Mountains. It also is called prairie-fire. The flower usually is a brilliant orange-red color but also can be yellow.

## WATER TUPELOS

Water tupelo trees commonly grow in the swampy and marshy areas of southeastern Arkansas. They can reach a height of 90 feet. The name tupelo comes from a Creek Indian phrase that means "tree and swamp."

**Black-eyed Susans** are yellow-and-black wildflowers that are found by roadsides and in fields throughout Arkansas from spring to fall.

**Bald cypress trees** are found along waterways and bayous throughout much of the southern United States. They often grow to be as tall as 120 feet. Their wood is very durable.

# Animals

rkansas's many natural areas provide homes for a wide variety of animals. Opossums, muskrats, weasels, rabbits, and squirrels can all be found in the state. Red and gray foxes also roam throughout Arkansas. Government game **refuges** maintain deer and elk populations in the state. The highland regions are home to black bears and bobcats. White-tailed deer and the **endangered** red-cockaded woodpecker live in the pine forests of southern Arkansas.

The wetlands of the Mississippi Delta region by the state's eastern border are an important winter haven for migrating birds. White River National Wildlife Refuge provides a winter home for Canada geese and mallard ducks. Some of the birds rest and feed in the fields before flying farther south toward the Gulf of Mexico.

**WHITE-TAILED DEER**

The white-tailed deer is the state mammal of Arkansas. This animal raises the white underside of its tail when frightened.

**MOCKINGBIRD**

Arkansas's state bird is the mockingbird. This bird mocks, or imitates, the songs of many other birds.

## RED-COCKADED WOODPECKER

This type of woodpecker is very rare and lives only in old-growth pine forests. It was declared an endangered species in 1970.

## BOBCAT

The bobcat, a close relative of the lynx, roams the mountains of Arkansas.

**The honeybee** is Arkansas's state insect. A picture of a dome beehive can be found on the Great Seal of Arkansas.

**Due to overhunting**, Arkansas's black bear population was once in jeopardy. The animals were successfully reintroduced in the state in the 1950s and 1960s.

# Tourism

**W**hether they go to Arkansas to enjoy the great outdoors or to learn about U.S. history, visitors will not be disappointed. There is much to see and do. The Natural State's many attractions draw more than 20 million tourists and bring in more than $5 billion each year.

The state capital, Little Rock, is a good place to begin a tour of Arkansas. Little Rock has many historic sites for visitors to enjoy. The Old State House was home to Arkansas's government from 1836 to 1911. Today the building is a historical museum.

Beyond Little Rock, tourists flock to the mountains to enjoy hiking, camping, and fishing. The Ozark and Ouachita Mountains are especially popular for their beautiful scenery. Arkansas also offers many natural hot springs. Bubbling hot springs can be found in the towns of Eureka Springs and Hot Springs. After a day of sightseeing, people can soak their travel-weary muscles in these soothing waters.

## OLD STATE HOUSE MUSEUM

Visitors to Little Rock can see the Old State House Museum, which features exhibits on the state's history.

## HOT SPRINGS NATIONAL PARK

People have been visiting Hot Springs, southwest of Little Rock, for more than 200 years for relaxation and to treat illnesses.

## OUACHITA NATIONAL FOREST

Situated mainly in the mountains of west-central Arkansas, the Ouachita National Forest is the oldest and largest national forest in the South. It covers 1.8 million acres of land.

## WILLIAM J. CLINTON PRESIDENTIAL CENTER AND PARK

The Clinton Center opened in 2004 in Little Rock. It features a library and museum devoted to Bill Clinton, the 42nd U.S. president.

# I DIDN'T KNOW THAT!

**At Eureka Springs** visitors can see the 70-foot statue "Christ of the Ozarks" or watch an outdoor Passion play depicting Christ's final days on Earth.

**The Ozark Folk Center** in Mountain View preserves the unique music, crafts, and folklore of the people of the Ozarks.

**The Pea Ridge** National Military Park is located in the northeastern corner of Arkansas on the site of a historic Civil War battle that took place in March 1862.

**The Bradley County** Pink Tomato Festival is held each June in Warren. About 30,000 people attend the weeklong event every year.

# Industry

Agriculture has always been important to the economy of Arkansas. Watermelons, grapes, blueberries, and apples are all grown in the state. Of all the crops that grow in Arkansas, rice is the most important. Arkansas produces more than twice as much rice as any other state.

## Industries in Arkansas
### Value of Goods and Services in Millions of Dollars

Manufacturing brings in more money than almost any other sector of Arkansas's economy. Can you name some manufactured products that you use regularly?

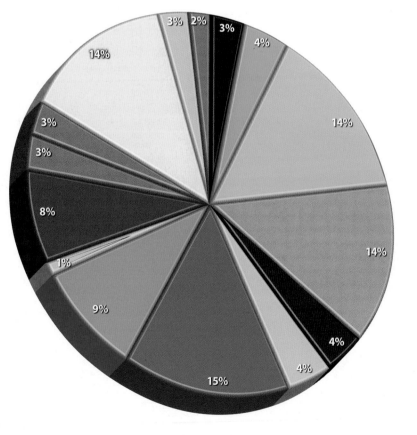

Percentages do not add to 100 because of rounding.

**LEGEND**

| Agriculture, Forestry, and Fishing | $2,870 |
| Mining | $2,039 |
| Utilities | $2,593 |
| Construction | $4,219 |
| Manufacturing | $14,632 |
| Wholesale and Retail Trade | $14,107 |
| Transportation | $4,394 |
| Media and Entertainment | $4,470 |
| Finance, Insurance, and Real Estate | $15,292 |
| Professional and Technical Services | $8,943 |
| Education | $512 |
| Health Care | $7,806 |
| Hotels and Restaurants | $2,610 |
| Other Services | $2,627 |
| Government | $14,702 |
| **TOTAL** | **$101,818** |

In the plains of eastern Arkansas, farmers grow rice in flat fields. Young rice plants must be kept wet. Farmers build earthen banks around their fields and then pump in enough water to cover the plants. The rice plants are submerged under 2 to 6 inches of water until the grain starts to ripen. Then the water is drained and the rice is harvested.

Chickens are another valuable farm product. Arkansas leads nearly all other states in poultry production. The state's farmers raise more than 1 billion chickens each year. Most are raised for their meat, others for their eggs. Every year Arkansas chickens produce more than 3 billion eggs.

In addition to agriculture, Arkansas has a large manufacturing industry. Electrical equipment, chemicals, machinery and other metal products, and goods made of paper, wood, rubber, and plastic are all produced in the state.

Other important industries in the state include wholesale and retail trade, finance, insurance, real estate, and professional and technical services.

*Food processing is a leading source of manufacturing jobs in Arkansas.*

I DIDN'T KNOW THAT!

**Little Rock and Fort Smith** are Arkansas's leading industrial areas.

**Leather and textile** production are important industries in the state.

**Berryville** is the self-proclaimed Turkey Capital. The town raises many thousands of turkeys each year.

**Stuttgart** is known as the Rice and Duck Capital of the World. The town is the seat of Arkansas County, which grows more rice than any other U.S. county.

**The flat-bottomed boats** called barges are commonly used for shipping goods on the state's many rivers.

# Goods and Services

A rkansas's workforce is made up of more than 1.3 million people. The largest number of them work in the service sector. This part of the economy is made up of jobs in a great variety of fields, including health care, real estate, trade, and transportation. One important part of the service sector in Arkansas is education. The people who provide educational services include teachers, principals, and college instructors. Arkansas has more than 1,000 public schools and more than 200 private schools. There are also 22 four-year colleges and 22 two-year colleges. Hospitality and tourism workers provide services, too. They work in restaurants, hotels, and tourist information centers.

Government workers are also considered part of the service sector. They make up about 16 percent of the state's workforce. Not all government employees work in office buildings. Some work in Arkansas's three national forests or 52 state parks. These people include rangers and wardens. Other government workers include military soldiers and civil servants. Many of these civil servants work in the state capital, Little Rock.

More than 465,000 students attend public schools in Arkansas.

In the past Arkansas's economy relied on agricultural goods. Today many different types of companies are doing business in the state. Arkansas has the home offices of a number of large companies, including Tyson Foods, Riceland Foods, ALLTEL, Dillard's, and J.B. Hunt Transport Services. Stephens Incorporated, based in Little Rock, is one of the largest investment firms in the country outside New York City.

One of the most famous goods providers in the United States originated in Arkansas. The Wal-Mart chain of stores sells a variety of items, from clothing to toys to household appliances. The company was founded by Sam Walton, who lived from 1918 to 1992. The first Wal-Mart opened in Rogers, Arkansas, in 1962. By 1991 Wal-Mart had become the largest retail chain in the world.

About 4,500 government employees work at Little Rock Air Force Base.

# I DIDN'T KNOW THAT!

**The L'Oréal cosmetics company** employs about 700 people at its facility in North Little Rock.

**The Dillard's department** store chain employs about 2,400 people at its headquarters in Little Rock.

**Tyson Foods** in Springdale is the world's largest processor and marketer of chicken, beef, and pork.

**Arkansas Industrial University** opened in Fayetteville in 1871. It later became the University of Arkansas.

**More than 700** Wal-Mart stores are located across the United States. The company is based in Bentonville.

# American Indians

**A**rchaeologists believe that people have lived in the Arkansas area for at least 12,000 years. The first inhabitants in the area were hunter-gatherers who lived in caves. Later inhabitants of the region were part of the Mississippian culture, which thrived from around the year 800 to the time of European exploration. The Mississippian people built huge earthen mounds and cultivated corn, beans, squash, and other crops. Many of these people lived in towns along rivers.

From 1838 to 1839, Cherokee Indians were made to travel across northern Arkansas on their way to Indian Territory. This route has become known as the Trail of Tears.

At the time of European settlement, three main groups of American Indians lived in the area. The Osage were hunters in northern Arkansas, the Caddo lived along the Red River in the southern part of the state, and the Quapaw built villages at the mouth of the Arkansas River. These peoples grew pumpkins and corn and hunted wild animals. During the early 1800s they had to give up much of their land to white settlers. The government forced the American Indians to leave Arkansas and other parts of the southeast. Many of them were relocated to Indian Territory, in what is now Oklahoma.

## I DIDN'T KNOW THAT!

**Early American Indians** known as **Bluff** Dwellers lived in caves along the White River. They made their homes under rock shelves.

**The Quapaw** were skilled artisans noted for their red-on-white pottery.

**The Toltec Mounds** near Little Rock are the tallest dirt mounds built by American Indians in Arkansas. The largest of the mounds is 49 feet high. The mounds are believed to have been used for religious ceremonies and burials.

**Osage Indians** lived in northwestern Arkansas. Osage women foraged for edible plants and raised crops such as squash, corn, and beans. Osage men hunted for a variety of animals, including buffalo, deer, antelope, and bear.

*More than 100 mounds built by prehistoric Indians of the Mississippian culture have been found throughout Arkansas.*

# Explorers and Missionaries

The Spanish explorer Hernando de Soto was the first European to come to the Arkansas region. He arrived in 1541 during an unsuccessful **expedition** for gold. Two Frenchmen, Louis Jolliet and Father Jacques Marquette, visited the area 132 years later. They canoed down the Mississippi River and reached the Arkansas River in 1673. Marquette was a missionary who wanted to teach Christianity to the American Indians, and Jolliet was a fur trader and mapmaker.

Explorer Henri de Tonti was born in Italy in 1649 and grew up in France. While traveling through the Mississippi Valley in 1686 he established the historic Arkansas Post settlement, which earned him the nickname the Father of Arkansas. He died in 1704 in what is now Mobile, Alabama.

In 1682 the French explorer René-Robert Cavelier, sieur de La Salle, arrived at the mouth of the Mississippi River. He claimed all of the Mississippi Valley for France. La Salle called this region Louisiana in honor of the king of France, Louis XIV. Arkansas was included in this territory.

La Salle's lieutenant, Henri de Tonti, established Arkansas Post in 1686. This fur-trading post was the first European settlement in what is now Arkansas. That is why Tonti is known as the Father of Arkansas.

# Timeline of Settlement

## Early Exploration and Colonization

**1541** Spanish conqueror Hernando de Soto leads the first European expedition into Arkansas.

**1673** Louis Jolliet and Father Jacques Marquette travel south on the Mississippi River. They turn back north the next year after reaching the mouth of the Arkansas River.

**1682** René-Robert Cavelier, sieur de La Salle, claims the Mississippi Valley for King Louis XIV of France, naming the country "Louisiana."

**1686** Arkansas Post is established as a trading post by La Salle's lieutenant, Henri de Tonti.

**1762** A secret treaty gives parts of Louisiana, including what is now Arkansas, to Spain. Thirty-eight years later, another secret agreement will return the region to French control.

## Establishment as a U.S. Territory

**1803** The French government sells the Louisiana Territory to the United States for $15 million. The deal, known as the Louisiana Purchase, makes what is now Arkansas part of the United States.

**1804–1815** The U.S. government approves various measures to survey and divide the Louisiana Territory and promote settlement of its lands.

**1819** President James Monroe signs an act of Congress creating the Territory of Arkansas.

**1821** The territorial government moves from Arkansas Post to Little Rock.

## Statehood and Civil War

**1836** Arkansas becomes the 25th state of the Union on June 15. James Conway is elected its first governor.

**1861** Arkansas secedes from, or leaves, the Union and joins the Confederacy.

**1861–1865** The people of Arkansas have divided loyalties during the Civil War. Some 50,000 join the Confederate army, while 15,000 fight for the Union.

**1865** The Confederacy is defeated by the Union, and the Civil War ends.

**1868** Arkansas is readmitted to the Union as a state.

# Early Settlers

**D**uring the 1700s European settlement in the Arkansas region was slow to develop. In 1762 France turned over the Louisiana Territory to Spain. The Spanish government offered free land and tax incentives to encourage settlement in the area. Largely unsuccessful in developing the region, Spain returned the territory to France.

## Map of Settlements and Resources in Early Arkansas

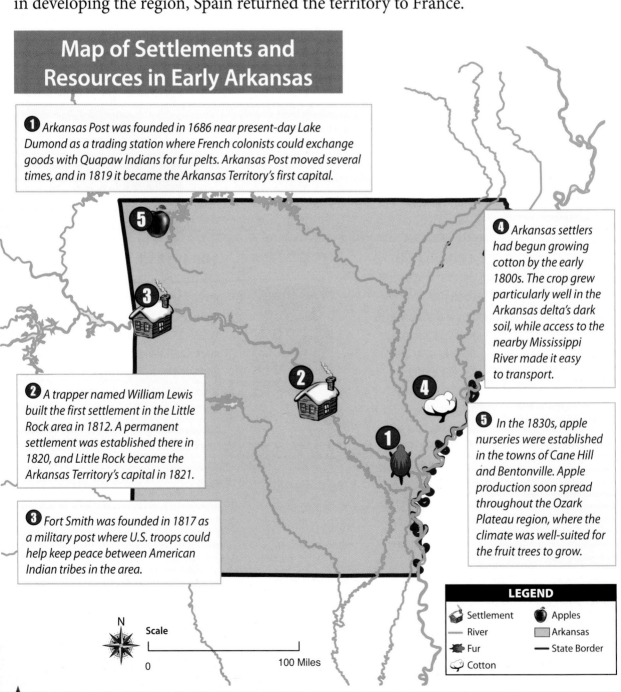

**1** Arkansas Post was founded in 1686 near present-day Lake Dumond as a trading station where French colonists could exchange goods with Quapaw Indians for fur pelts. Arkansas Post moved several times, and in 1819 it became the Arkansas Territory's first capital.

**4** Arkansas settlers had begun growing cotton by the early 1800s. The crop grew particularly well in the Arkansas delta's dark soil, while access to the nearby Mississippi River made it easy to transport.

**2** A trapper named William Lewis built the first settlement in the Little Rock area in 1812. A permanent settlement was established there in 1820, and Little Rock became the Arkansas Territory's capital in 1821.

**5** In the 1830s, apple nurseries were established in the towns of Cane Hill and Bentonville. Apple production soon spread throughout the Ozark Plateau region, where the climate was well-suited for the fruit trees to grow.

**3** Fort Smith was founded in 1817 as a military post where U.S. troops could help keep peace between American Indian tribes in the area.

**N**

**Scale**

0        100 Miles

### LEGEND

| | | | |
|---|---|---|---|
| 🥁 | Settlement | 🍎 | Apples |
| — | River | ▨ | Arkansas |
| 🦫 | Fur | ▬ | State Border |
| 🌱 | Cotton | | |

In 1803 the United States bought the Louisiana Territory from France. The land that is now Arkansas was included in this deal. In the years that followed thousands of settlers moved into the Arkansas region. They built log cabins and planted vegetables and fruit trees. Many settlers farmed in central Arkansas and the northern hills, and some began cultivating apples in the northwest. Others started growing cotton and tobacco in the rich **bottomlands** of the southeast. Many slaves were taken to Arkansas to work the cotton plantations along the Mississippi River. Slavery was legal in the Southern states until the end of the Civil War in 1865.

While most early settlers lived on farms and plantations, new towns began to form as well. Hot Springs was founded in 1807.

The town of Fort Smith began as a U.S. Army post in 1817. Arkansas became a territory in 1819. Little Rock was founded the next year, and became Arkansas's capital in 1821. In 1836 the territory's population reached 60,000 people, the number required for statehood. In that year Arkansas became the 25th state in the United States.

*Arkansas had a population of 435,000 in 1860. One-fourth of the people were black slaves.*

# I DIDN'T KNOW THAT!

**Today** people can visit the Arkansas Post National Memorial on the site of Henri de Tonti's original settlement.

**In 1800** fewer than 400 people of European heritage lived in what is now Arkansas.

**In 1811 and 1812** earthquakes along the New Madrid Fault rocked northeastern Arkansas.

**In 1835 Davy Crockett** passed through Arkansas on his way to Texas. A dinner was given in his honor in Little Rock.

**Arkansas** experienced a huge population boom between 1820 and 1840, when more than 80,000 new settlers arrived in the region.

**Two major battles** were fought in Arkansas during the Civil War, at Pea Ridge and Prairie Grove.

# Notable People

**M**any people who were born and lived in Arkansas have made important contributions to the state, the country, and even the world. Here are just a few Arkansans whose accomplishments had a positive influence on others.

**BILL CLINTON
(1946– )**

Clinton was born in Hope and grew up in Hot Springs. In 1978 he became governor of Arkansas at age 32, making him the youngest person ever to be elected a U.S. governor. Clinton was elected the 42nd president of the United States in 1992 and served two terms. Following his presidency, Clinton has served his country as a diplomat, statesman, and philanthropist.

**DOUGLAS MacARTHUR
(1880–1964)**

Born in Little Rock, MacArthur was one of the most famous U.S. generals of the 20th century. His many achievements include helping to lead the United States and its allies to victory in the Pacific during World World II and serving as supreme commander of the Allied Powers in the postwar occupation of Japan. MacArthur also commanded U.S. troops in the Korean War, until dismissed by President Harry Truman for publicly disagreeing with Truman's policies.

## J. WILLIAM FULBRIGHT (1905–1995)

Fulbright, who grew up in Fayetteville, spent almost 30 years as a U.S. senator. During that time he became known for promoting cultural tolerance and international cooperation. In 1946, he established the Fulbright scholarship program, which allows American students and educators to study abroad.

## JOHN H. JOHNSON (1918–2005)

Johnson was born in Arkansas City, Arkansas, but moved to Chicago before he began high school. In 1942, he founded the Johnson Publishing Company, which has become the largest African-American-owned media company in the world. It publishes two very popular African-American-oriented magazines, *Ebony* and *Jet*.

## HATTIE CARAWAY (1878–1950)

Caraway was a Jonesboro resident when her husband, Thaddeus, became a U.S. senator in 1921. When he died in 1931, Hattie was appointed by Arkansas's governor to fill the position. After winning a special election in 1932, she became the first woman ever elected to the U.S. Senate. She spent 13 years in Congress.

## I DIDN'T KNOW THAT!

**Edward Durell Stone (1902–1978)**, who was born and raised in Fayetteville, became one of the most renowned architects of his time. His work includes the University of Arkansas for Medical Sciences Medical Center in Little Rock and the John F. Kennedy Center for the Performing Arts in Washington, D.C.

**Daisy Gatson Bates (c. 1913–1999)** and her husband published an African-American-oriented newspaper in Little Rock. She became a mentor and supporter of the Little Rock Nine, a group of African American students who in 1957 **integrated** the city's Central High School in the face of angry protestors who favored **segregation**.

# Population

With more than 2.9 million people, Arkansas is the 32nd largest state in population. Arkansas has always been an agricultural state, with a great number of people living in **rural** areas. About 40 percent of the population lives on farms or in other rural settings.

## Arkansas Population 1950–2010

Arkansas's population has increased steadily for most of the past 60 years. During what decade did the state's population decrease? What factors may have caused this decline?

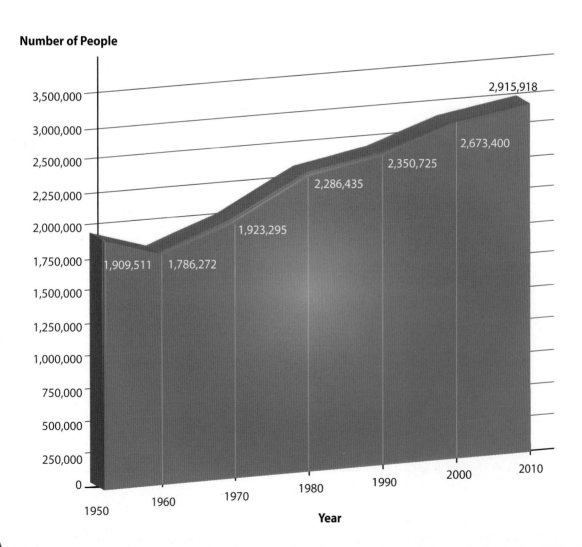

**Number of People**

- 1950: 1,909,511
- 1960: 1,786,272
- 1970: 1,923,295
- 1980: 2,286,435
- 1990: 2,350,725
- 2000: 2,673,400
- 2010: 2,915,918

**Year**

More than 1 million people reside in rural areas of Arkansas.

Most of the cities in Arkansas are small. Little Rock is the largest city in Arkansas, with a population of more than 188,000. As the state capital, Little Rock is a center for government, education, transportation, and culture. Little Rock also has a "twin city" across the Arkansas River. This city, North Little Rock, has a population of almost 60,000. Other major cities in Arkansas include Fort Smith, Pine Bluff, Fayetteville, Springdale, Jonesboro, and Hot Springs.

# I DIDN'T KNOW THAT!

**Arkansas** is divided into 75 counties.

**The University of Arkansas** is located in Fayetteville, which is the third-largest city in the state.

**Two cities named Texarkana** lie next to each other on either side of the Texas-Arkansas border. Texarkana, Texas, has about 36,000 people, while Texarkana, Arkansas, has about 30,000.

The small town of Helena draws many thousands of people to its annual Arkansas Blues and Heritage Festival.

# Politics and Government

L aws and important decisions that affect all Arkansans are made in Little Rock. The state government is composed of three branches. The executive branch approves and administers laws. The legislative branch introduces new laws and changes existing ones. The judicial branch is composed of the state courts.

Arkansas's present State Capitol was built from 1899 to 1915. It sits on a hilltop west of downtown Little Rock. The building has large columns and a grand staircase, all made of marble.

The state legislature, or General Assembly, consists of the Senate and the House of Representatives. The Senate has 35 members, and the House of Representatives has 100. On the federal level, two senators and four members of the House of Representatives represent Arkansas in the U.S. Congress in Washington, D.C.

Bill Clinton is a well-known political figure from Arkansas. He was elected governor of Arkansas in 1978 and served the state in this role for many years. Clinton then served as the president of the United States from 1993 to 2001. Another notable Arkansas politician is Mike Huckabee. He was governor from 1996 to 2007, and unsuccessfully competed for the Republican presidential nomination in 2008.

# I DIDN'T KNOW THAT!

**Arkansas has four state songs. One of these, "Arkansas" by Eva Ware Barnett, was designated the state's official anthem in 1987.**

Here is an excerpt from the song:

*I am thinking tonight of the Southland,*
*Of the home of my childhood days,*
*Where I roamed through the woods and the meadows,*
*By the mill and the brook that plays*

*Arkansas, Arkansas, 'tis a name dear,*
*'Tis the place I call "home, sweet home,"*
*Arkansas, Arkansas, I salute thee,*
*From thy shelter no more I'll roam*

*After serving as the governor of Arkansas and president of the United States, Bill Clinton has undertaken a variety of humanitarian projects. These include working for the United Nations to help Haiti rebuild following the major earthquake that hit the country in 2010.*

# Cultural Groups

About four-fifths of Arkansans are of European heritage. European settlers arrived in the state from Ireland, Germany, Great Britain, and many other countries. Some of these newcomers settled in the Ozark Mountains. They created a rich folk culture with their own arts, crafts, music, and dances. These people lived in remote areas and often had very little money. They were **resourceful** and made many things by hand instead of buying them. The Ozark Folk Center in Mountain View works to preserve the cultural traditions of this region. There visitors can see craftspeople making various useful household items. Local musicians may be seen at the Ozark Folk Center playing folk songs on the traditional instruments of this musical style, including fiddles, banjos, and guitars.

The people of the Ozark Mountains are known for crafting handmade items such as wood carvings, baskets, quilts, and candles.

In 1957 Little Rock's Central High School received its first nine African American students. The students, remembered as the Little Rock Nine, entered the school under the protection of federal troops. The students were later awarded the Congressional Gold Medal for their contributions to U.S. civil rights.

African Americans are another important cultural group in Arkansas, making up about 16 percent of the population. When the first Africans were taken to Arkansas in the late 1700s, most of them were forced to work as slaves on plantations. Today, after many social reforms in the United States, African Americans participate in every area of society. Every February, Arkansas celebrates Black History Month. This is a time for African Americans to share and preserve their history and culture. Many people reflect on African Americans' long struggle for civil rights in the United States. In Little Rock, the Central High Museum and Visitor's Center honors the first African American students who struggled against segregation in the state's schools.

At the time of European settlement, a number of American Indian groups lived in the Arkansas area. In the years leading up to statehood in 1836, many American Indians were forced to move out of the region. Today American Indians account for only a small number of the state's residents. In total, there are some 25,000 American Indians living in Arkansas.

# I DIDN'T KNOW THAT!

**The square dance** is Arkansas's official state folk dance.

**Juneteenth** is celebrated on June 19 in many cities across Arkansas. On this day African Americans mark the end of slavery in the Southern states.

**The Arkansas State Old-Time Fiddle Contest** is held every autumn at the Ozark Folk Center in Mountain View.

**In Pine Bluff** there are a dozen murals that depict the city's history and culture.

**The Delta Cultural Center** in Helena is a museum dedicated to the history and music of Arkansas's delta region.

# Arts and Entertainment

**A**rkansas boasts a thriving arts scene. Many people in the state use art, music, and the written word to share their ideas and experiences with others.

Country music is a prominent part of Arkansas's arts and entertainment scene. Many well-known artists have come from the state. Johnny Cash, born in Kingsland, was a very popular and influential singer whose nickname was the Man in Black. His hits included "I Walk the Line" and "Folsom Prison Blues." Glen Campbell is a native of Delight. He has had many hit records and hosted his own television variety show.

Conway Twitty was known as the High Priest of Country Music. He was raised in Helena, where he was known as Harold Jenkins. His stage name combines the names of two towns: Conway, Arkansas, and Twitty, Texas.

Arkansas also has produced famous musicians who are known for other styles of music. Ne-Yo is a chart-topping R&B artist who sings, raps, and dances. He was born in Camden, and his given name is Shaffer Chimere Smith. Forrest City native Al Green is a renowned soul and gospel singer. Louis Jordan was a pioneer of jazz, blues, and R&B. He was born in Brinkley.

*Legendary singer-songwriter Johnny Cash (1932–2003) was inducted into the Country Music Hall of Fame in 1980 and the Rock and Roll Hall of Fame in 1992.*

R&B singer Ne-Yo's first three albums all sold more than 1 million copies. The multitalented artist is also a record producer, dancer, and actor.

Some acclaimed writers also have come from Arkansas. John Grisham, who was born in Jonesboro, writes legal thrillers. His many novels include *The Firm*, *The Pelican Brief*, and *The Client*. Many of Grisham's novels have been made into successful movies.

Maya Angelou, who grew up in Stamps, has won national recognition as a poet, novelist, actress, educator, and civil-rights activist. She is best known for her book *I Know Why the Caged Bird Sings*, which tells of her childhood experiences in Arkansas.

Arkansas offers numerous cultural attractions. Little Rock has many of the state's theaters, museums, and musical venues. The Arkansas Symphony, Ballet Arkansas, and the Arkansas Arts Center are all based in Little Rock.

**The fiddle** is Arkansas's state instrument.

**Singer Kris Allen**, from Conway, was named winner of the popular TV talent competition *American Idol* in 2009.

**WOK in Pine Bluff** was Arkansas's first radio station. It began broadcasting in 1922.

**The television station KATV** in Little Rock began broadcasting in 1953.

**The actors** Mary Steenburgen and Billy Bob Thornton are both from Arkansas.

**Arkansas's first newspaper** was the *Arkansas Gazette*. It was founded by William E. Woodruff at Arkansas Post in 1819.

# Sports

With its mountains, streams, and beautiful scenery, the Natural State is the perfect place for outdoor sports and activities. Arkansas has more than 200 public campgrounds and many more private ones. There are countless day hikes, mountain bike paths, and **equestrian** trails to enjoy. People can even explore underground caves. Serious hikers can take an extended backpacking trip on the Ozark Highlands National Recreation Trail.

Bikers will enjoy touring the mountains and valleys of northern Arkansas. This region has some of the most scenic and physically challenging bike tours in the United States. Bikers can also explore bike routes in the Mississippi Valley. They will find both hills and level stretches in this area.

The University of Arkansas Razorbacks football team's current nickname was coined in 1909 by coach Hugo Bezdek, who said after one game that his squad played "like a wild band of razorback hogs."

Fishing and hunting are also popular pastimes in Arkansas. People can travel the more than 9,000 miles of streams in the state by canoe, **johnboat**, or raft. Known as a fisher's haven, these waterways provide some of the world's best fishing. Bass, walleye, and many kinds of trout are found in them.

Many people take advantage of the golf courses found all over Arkansas. Golfers can find courses in the mountains and in the delta region. Because of the warm climate, golfers in Arkansas can tee off year-round.

Many Arkansans enjoy watching and playing team sports. The University of Arkansas sports teams are known as the Razorbacks after a type of wild hog native to the area. Football is especially popular in the state. The Razorbacks football team has won many postseason games, including the Orange Bowl, the Sugar Bowl, and the Cotton Bowl. The Razorbacks men's basketball team won the national title in 1994.

With more than 600,000 acres of lakes and 9,700 miles of rivers and streams, Arkansas is a haven for fishing enthusiasts.

## I DIDN'T KNOW THAT!

**Jay Hanna (Dizzy) Dean**, born in Lucas, Arkansas, was a hard-throwing pitcher who was elected to the Baseball Hall of Fame in 1953. For many years Dizzy Dean and his brother Paul Dee (Daffy) Dean pitched for the St. Louis Cardinals.

**Cliff Lee, a Benton native**, has been a star pitcher for several Major League Baseball teams. He won the Cy Young Award in 2008 as a member of the Cleveland Indians, and he pitched in the World Series in 2009 with the Philadelphia Phillies and 2010 with the Texas Rangers.

**Scottie Pippen** was a basketball star at Central Arkansas University. He later played for the Chicago Bulls and helped them win NBA championships in 1991, 1992, 1993, 1996, 1997, and 1998.

# National Averages Comparison

T he United States is a federal republic, consisting of fifty states and the District of Columbia. Alaska and Hawai'i are the only non-contiguous, or non-touching, states in the nation. Today, the United States of America is the third-largest country in the world in population. The United States Census Bureau takes a census, or count of all the people, every ten years. It also regularly collects other kinds of data about the population and the economy. How does Arkansas compare to the national average?

## Comparison Chart

| United States 2010 Census Data * | USA | Arkansas |
|---|---|---|
| Admission to Union | NA | June 15, 1836 |
| Land Area (in square miles) | 3,537,438.44 | 52,068.17 |
| Population Total | 308,745,538 | 2,915,918 |
| Population Density (people per square mile) | 87.28 | 56.00 |
| Population Percentage Change (April 1, 2000, to April 1, 2010) | 9.7% | 9.1% |
| White Persons (percent) | 72.4% | 77.0% |
| Black Persons (percent) | 12.6% | 15.4% |
| American Indian and Alaska Native Persons (percent) | 0.9% | 0.8% |
| Asian Persons (percent) | 4.8% | 1.2% |
| Native Hawaiian and Other Pacific Islander Persons (percent) | 0.2% | 0.2% |
| Some Other Race (percent) | 6.2% | 3.4% |
| Persons Reporting Two or More Races (percent) | 2.9% | 2.0% |
| Persons of Hispanic or Latino Origin (percent) | 16.3% | 6.4% |
| Not of Hispanic or Latino Origin (percent) | 83.7% | 93.6% |
| Median Household Income | $52,029 | $38,820 |
| Percentage of People Age 25 or Over Who Have Graduated from High School | 80.4% | 75.3% |

*All figures are based on the 2010 United States Census, with the exception of the last three items.

# How to Improve My Community

Strong communities make strong states. Think about what features are important in your community. What do you value? Education? Health? Forests? Safety? Beautiful spaces? Government works to help citizens create ideal living conditions that are fair to all by providing services in communities. Consider what changes you could make in your community. How would they improve your state as a whole? Using this concept web as a guide, write a report that outlines the features you think are most important in your community and what improvements could be made. A strong state needs strong communities.

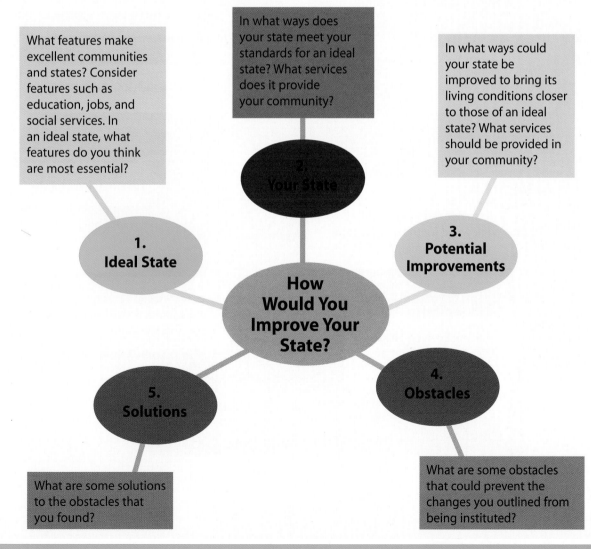

What features make excellent communities and states? Consider features such as education, jobs, and social services. In an ideal state, what features do you think are most essential?

In what ways does your state meet your standards for an ideal state? What services does it provide your community?

In what ways could your state be improved to bring its living conditions closer to those of an ideal state? What services should be provided in your community?

2.
Your State

1.
Ideal State

3.
Potential
Improvements

How
Would You
Improve Your
State?

5.
Solutions

4.
Obstacles

What are some solutions to the obstacles that you found?

What are some obstacles that could prevent the changes you outlined from being instituted?

# Exercise Your Mind!

Think about these questions and then use your research skills to find the answers and learn more fascinating facts about Arkansas. A teacher, librarian, or parent may be able to help you locate the best sources to use in your research.

**1** How did the town of Texarkana get its name?

**2** What is the rock in the name Little Rock?

**3** Mountain View, known for its authentic mountain music, is renowned for the manufacture of what instrument?

**4** What are Evening Shade, Okay, Toad Suck, Tomato, and Strawberry?

**5** Rearrange the following series of words to make a four-word phrase that relates to the subject of this book: SNAKES TARANTULAS AT HEART.

**6** Who were the Little Rock Nine?

**7** What is a "fried pie"?

**8** What interesting artifacts can be found at Arkansas's Hampson Museum?

# Words to Know

**bayous:** marshy arms of a lake or river

**bluff:** a cliff or steep riverbank

**bottomlands:** low-lying lands around a waterway

**endangered:** in danger of dying out

**equestrian:** involving horses or horseback riding

**expedition:** a journey of exploration

**integrated:** brought people of different races together

**johnboat:** a narrow, flat-bottomed boat used on rivers and streams

**plantations:** large farms that are usually tended by resident workers

**refuges:** places of shelter and protection

**resourceful:** able to invent new ways to do or make things in difficult situations

**rural:** of or relating to life in the country or on farms

**segregation:** forced separation and restrictions based on race

# Index

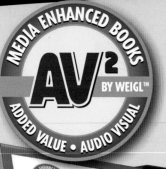

# Log on to www.av2books.com

AV[2] by Weigl brings you media enhanced books that support active learning. Go to www.av2books.com, and enter the special code found on page 2 of this book. You will gain access to enriched and enhanced content that supplements and complements this book. Content includes video, audio, web links, quizzes, a slide show, and activities.

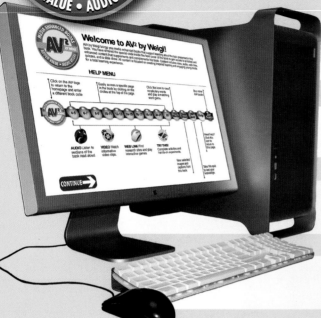

### Audio
Listen to sections of the book read aloud.

### Video
Watch informative video clips.

### Embedded Weblinks
Gain additional information for research.

### Try This!
Complete activities and hands-on experiments.

# WHAT'S ONLINE?

|  Try This! |  Embedded Weblinks |  Video | EXTRA FEATURES |
|---|---|---|---|
| Test your knowledge of the state in a mapping activity. | Discover more attractions in Arkansas. | Watch a video introduction to Arkansas. |  **Audio** Listen to sections of the book read aloud. |
| Find out more about precipitation in your city. | Learn more about the history of the state. | Watch a video about the features of the state. |  **Key Words** Study vocabulary, and complete a matching word activity. |
| Plan what attractions you would like to visit in the state. | Learn the full lyrics of the state song. | | |
| Learn more about the early natural resources of the state. | | |  **Slide Show** View images and captions, and prepare a presentation. |
| Write a biography about a notable resident of Arkansas. | | | |
| Complete an educational census activity. | | |  **Quizzes** Test your knowledge. |

AV[2] was built to bridge the gap between print and digital. We encourage you to tell us what you like and what you want to see in the future.

## Sign up to be an AV[2] Ambassador at www.av2books.com/ambassador.

Due to the dynamic nature of the Internet, some of the URLs and activities provided as part of AV[2] by Weigl may have changed or ceased to exist. AV[2] by Weigl accepts no responsibility for any such changes. All media enhanced books are regularly monitored to update addresses and sites in a timely manner. Contact AV[2] by Weigl at 1-866-649-3445 or av2books@weigl.com with any questions, comments, or feedback.